THE HISTORY OF IMMIGRATION

CATHLEEN SMALL

LUCENT
PRESS

Published in 2018 by
Lucent Press, an Imprint of Greenhaven Publishing, LLC
353 3rd Avenue
Suite 255
New York, NY 10010

Produced for Lucent by Calcium
Designer: Jeni Child
Picture researcher: Rachel Blount
Editors: Sarah Eason and Nancy Dickmann

Picture credits: Cover: Shutterstock: Everett Historical (main), Vinokurov Kirill (top); Inside: Library of Congress: 30, Currier & Ives 7, Detroit Photographic Co. 32, Edmonston Studio 43, Leffler, Warren K., 46, 47, Underwood & Underwood 35, Gift; Carl Van Vechten Estate; 1966 44; Shutterstock: Bikeriderlondon 4, Paolo Bona 53, Marie Kanger Born 61, Dean Drobot 52, Emkaplin 45, Everett Historical 14, 18–19, 22, 23, 25t, 25b, 26–27, 28, 29, 31, 34, 37, 39, 40, Holbox 36, JStone 58, Somjin Klong-ugkara 51, Vladimir Korostyshevskiy 10, Mikeledray 59, Felix Mizioznikov 5, Rehan Qureshi 55, Joseph Sohm 56, Stocksnapper 12, Richard Thornton 49, Vkilikov 6; Wikimedia Commons: Internet Archive Book Images/Flickr API 11, Unknown printmaker after painting by unidentified "Kelley"; Copyright Silver, Burdett & Co. 20, Library of Congress 8, Howard Pyle 21, Robert Walter Weir 9.

Library of Congress Cataloging-in-Publication Data

Names: Small, Cathleen.
Title: The history of immigration / Cathleen Small.
Description: New York : Lucent Press, 2018. | Series: Crossing the border | Includes index.
Identifiers: ISBN 9781534562219 (library bound) | ISBN 9781534562226 (ebook) | ISBN 9781534562806 (paperback)
Subjects: LCSH: Immigrants--United States--History--Juvenile literature. | United States--Emigration and immigration--History--Juvenile literature.
Classification: LCC E184.A1 S63 2018 | DDC 304.80973--dc23

Printed in the United States of America

CPSIA compliance information: Batch #CW18KL: For further information contact Greenhaven Publishing LLC, New York, New York at 1-844-317-7404.

CONTENTS

CHAPTER 1

IMMIGRATION IN THE COLONIAL ERA

The United States is often described as a melting pot. This term dates from the late 18th century, but it became more widely used in 1908, when a play about Russian-Jewish immigrants opened in Washington, D.C. It was popular, and it gained the approval of President Theodore Roosevelt.

In reality, the United States has been a melting pot for a long time—the mixing of people began even before it was the United States! When Spanish expeditions reached the coast of the Americas in the late 15th century, the continents were already settled by a diverse population of Native American groups. The Spanish established some early colonies in the southern portion of North America. By the 17th century, England, France, Sweden, and the Dutch Republic had all established colonies in North America. North America was quickly becoming a diverse blend of backgrounds and cultures.

Every year, people from many different backgrounds come to the United States to seek citizenship.

4

Spanish Colonies in North America

The first official European settlement in North America was Spanish Florida, established in 1513. It included present-day Florida and much of what is now Georgia, Alabama, Mississippi, South Carolina, and Louisiana. The region was eventually filled with a diverse population. There were Spanish settlers, Native Americans from the local area, and Native Americans from northern regions, who had moved south when English settlers pushed them out of their lands. There were also African Americans who had escaped slavery in the English settlements. In a sense, it was a small melting pot within the much bigger melting pot of the United States.

ST. AUGUSTINE, FLORIDA

Many people think of the English colonies when considering the earliest European settlements in North America. However, the oldest one in the United States is actually Spanish. It is the city of St. Augustine, in Florida. It was founded in 1565 by Pedro Menéndez de Avilés, a Spanish conquistador, and it became the capital of Spanish Florida when the area was further settled. In 1819, Spain ceded Florida to the United States. St. Augustine was its capital for the first several years, until it was changed to Tallahassee. Modern-day St. Augustine is a quaint little town and a major Florida tourist attraction.

The Castillo de San Marcos in St. Augustine, Florida, is the oldest masonry fort in the United States.

SPANISH COLONIES

In the late 16th century, an expedition ordered by King Philip II of Spain resulted in the settlement of the province of Nuevo México. It covered an area that eventually became modern-day New Mexico, as well as parts of Texas, Colorado, Kansas, and Oklahoma. The goal of the Nuevo México settlement was to promote the spread of Catholicism, so much of the settlement evolved around the building of Spanish missions in the region.

« Spain reached a golden age under King Philip II, holding territories on every known continent at the time.

EARLY FRENCH COLONIES

Early French settlement in North America revolved around New France. This was a vast area that stretched from Canada and the northeastern part of what is now the United States, all the way through the plains of the Midwest and down to present-day Louisiana. One early area of settlement in this region was Acadia, which included territory in the far northeast of the current United States and Canada.

The French settlements did not remain under French rule for long, though. The settlements in Acadia and parts of Canada were established in the 17th century, but by the middle of the next century, France had lost most of its territories to England and Spain.

Swedish settlements

Although today Sweden is not known as a fierce military power, in the 17th century it was a fairly significant European country. Sweden established a number of colonies in North America between 1638 and 1655, mostly in the present-day states of Delaware, New Jersey, and Pennsylvania. The settlements were scattered along the Delaware River for trading purposes, and they were populated by Swedish, Finnish, and Dutch immigrants. However, by the end of the century, the colonies had all been taken over by the British. They were still largely composed of Scandinavian immigrants, but they were now under English rule.

Dutch settlers were lured to North America by the possibility of becoming rich from the fur trade.

Dutch colonies in the Northeast

In the 17th century, the Dutch established settlements in eastern North America, including portions of the present-day states of New York, New Jersey, Delaware, Connecticut, and Pennsylvania. The purpose of the Dutch settlements was to stake a Dutch claim in the North American fur trade. Because of this, the population included Dutch and other European settlers, Native Americans from the region, and African Americans who had been brought in as slaves to work in the fur industry. Much like Spanish Florida, it was an ethnically diverse region—a small melting pot within the bigger melting pot.

ENGLISH COLONIES

When people think of the early settlement of North America, two groups come to mind: the Native Americans who lived in the territory for thousands of years, and the English, who established some of the earliest settlements in North America. It was the English whose colonization rapidly expanded to form the colonies that ended up becoming the first 13 United States.

Native American groups populated North America long before English settlers ever arrived.

THE PILGRIMS

The first English colony was Jamestown, founded in 1607 in what is now the state of Virginia. In 1620, the Pilgrims arrived in Cape Cod (part of modern-day Massachusetts) after being unable to complete their journey to Virginia. The Pilgrims were English separatists seeking religious freedom, and they established Plymouth Colony in southeastern Massachusetts. Plymouth Colony was the first decent-sized English settlement in the northeastern United States. Many of the other English colonies, including Jamestown, were farther south, in Virginia.

THE PURITANS ARRIVE

Another wave of English settlers arrived starting in 1630. Like the Pilgrims, these settlers left England because of religious differences. They were Puritans, and their goal was to "purify" the Church of England. They felt that the Church of England had been tainted by Catholicism and needed reform. During a decade-long span known as the Great Migration, the Puritans founded the Massachusetts Bay Colony and other settlements in the area known as New England.

Artist Robert Walter Weir's painting showing the Pilgrims embarking on their voyage now hangs in the United States Capitol.

RELIGIOUS MIGRATION TO NORTH AMERICA

The Pilgrims and the Puritans both immigrated to North America seeking religious freedom, though in two different ways. The Puritans wanted to reform the Church of England and remove the Catholic influence from it, whereas the Pilgrims wanted to separate entirely from the Church of England. The religious beliefs of the two groups had some similarities, though. The Pilgrims also held Protestant beliefs (specifically, Calvinist), and neither group was in favor of Catholic practices. However, while the Puritans felt reform was an option, the Pilgrims felt a full separation from the Church of England was required.

So how many Puritans and Pilgrims immigrated to the colonies? It is estimated that around 21,000 Puritans came to the colonies during the Great Migration from 1630 to 1641. Although the term "pilgrim" technically refers to any person who moves to another place for religious reasons, the Pilgrims who settled Plymouth Colony are a specific group who sailed on the Mayflower in 1620, and they numbered 102.

MORE COLONIES

England went on to establish more colonies in the northeastern and mid-Atlantic areas of North America. Some colonies were founded by purchasing land from other countries' settlements. In other cases, the English settlers simply took the land over. They also set up some colonies in territories that had not yet been settled by Europeans.

Throughout the 17th and 18th centuries, up until the American Revolution began in 1775, England continued to expand their holdings in North America. In 1622, they gained control of the Province of Maine. The next year, they settled the Province of New Hampshire. Salem Colony was added in 1628, with the Massachusetts Bay Colony following in 1630. Connecticut Colony and the Province of Maryland came in 1633 and 1634, respectively, with Saybrook Colony following the next year. Rhode Island and Providence Plantations were both settled in 1636, and New Haven Colony was founded in 1638.

The Great Friends Meeting House in Newport, Rhode Island, is a good example of the simplicity that embodies the Quaker style.

THE QUAKERS

Although the Pilgrims and the Puritans are some of the best-known immigrants to come to North America seeking religious freedom, a third group did so as well. The Quaker religion was another breakaway group from the Church of England. Their belief system was based on Christianity, but was quite different from the belief structure of both the Pilgrims and the Puritans. Quakers encouraged a far more personal relationship with God than Pilgrim and Puritan religions did.

The Quaker religion had been established in England around the middle of the 17th century, and it immediately faced opposition and persecution. Looking for safety and religious freedom, Quakers began immigrating to North America in 1675. They poured into the Delaware Valley area and settled in West Jersey (now part of New Jersey), Rhode Island, and Pennsylvania. By 1750, Quakers were the third-largest religion in the colonies. The Quakers were also staunch abolitionists. They were the first organization in North America to ban the ownership of slaves.

Quakers were persecuted in England, but they found more religious freedom in North America.

TAKING OVER

The number of English settlements in North America continued to grow. England captured New York and New Jersey from the Dutch Republic in 1664. The Province of Pennsylvania was founded in 1681, and the Provinces of Carolina were settled soon after, as well as the Province of Georgia. In 1763, the English acquired territory in Florida from Spain.

COLONIES AND RICHES

European countries wanted colonies in North America because this new land was rich in natural resources. Many of the settlements were in areas with rich soil, and the fur trade prospered in the northeastern region. These new territories attracted immigrants from all over Europe because of the opportunities in the agricultural, fur, and shipping trades. The 17th and 18th centuries saw immigration of Dutch, Swedish, German, Scottish, and Scots–Irish peoples to North America. All of this colonization took place over a span of about 160 years. This may seem like rather a long time, but it actually represents a very quick spread of control.

The English systematically established colonies along the East Coast of North America, which was a very desirable area. There were many natural shipping ports along the East Coast and its associated waterways, meaning that goods could be easily shipped back to Europe. The English colonies, with their access to resources and ports, meant that the English were able to gain a powerful position in the region.

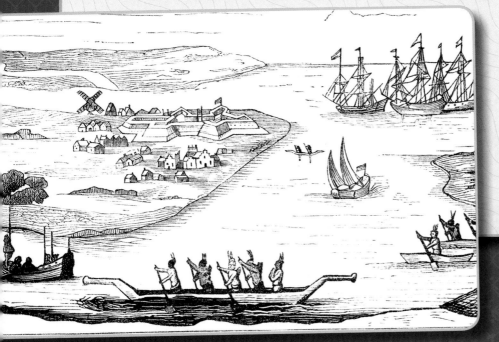

The Dutch who settled in the 17th century around what is now New York originally called the region "New Amsterdam."

EUROPEAN MIGRATION BY THE NUMBERS

A great number of English settlers immigrated to North America, but other European countries had significant numbers of immigrants as well. In the mid-17th century, approximately 10,000 Dutch and Belgian immigrants arrived to settle the territory of New Netherland (now the state of New York). Historians estimate that more than 48,000 people left Ireland for North America between 1750 and 1775. Approximately 25,000 Scottish people migrated to North America in just a 15-year span, from 1760 to 1775. Between 1700 and 1775, it is estimated that more than 84,000 Germans came to live in North America.

THE BEGINNING OF A NEW NATION

By the time the American Revolution began in 1775, the 13 colonies along the East Coast were settled. The quick development of trade in these new settlements also brought in another wave of immigrants, though these people did not immigrate by choice—they were slaves, brought by force from Africa and sold to local settlers.

Even before the war, the 13 colonies had a diverse population of immigrants from all over Europe and Africa, mixed with the local Native American people. It was quite the melting pot, even if the cultures were not quite "melting together" yet. Once the new nation of the United States was founded, immigration would continue to increase.

CHAPTER 2

INVOLUNTARY IMMIGRATION TO THE UNITED STATES

Much of the European immigration to North America was voluntary. People came of their own free will, seeking religious freedom or new opportunities. Many of them made a good living through farming or working in the fur and shipping trades. However, some people did not come to North America by choice.

Slaves were brought over from Africa and sold to white landowners in North America, who forced them to work without pay. Even some of the people who immigrated to North America by choice were forced to work in slave-like conditions, as indentured servants.

Slaves were brought to North America shortly after the first landowners settled there.

Indentured Servitude in the American Colonies

The first European immigrants to North America tended to be relatively wealthy. The passage to America by ship was expensive, and so people in the working classes often could not afford it. This meant that the earliest colonists were largely people who had at least a reasonable amount of money. When they landed in North America, they quickly settled in colonies with large plots of land. The problem soon became obvious: There was no one to work the land for them. These landowners needed workers, but manual laborers could not typically afford the cost of passage to North America.

The Terms of Indentured Servitude

The Virginia Company had been set up by King James I of England to establish settlements in North America. Its members thought of a solution: They would offer workers the chance to come to the colonies. However, their free passage came with the condition that they would work for four to seven years for an established settler before earning their full freedom in North America. This often included a sizable parcel of land, a year's worth of corn, new clothes, and weapons, so many workers thought it was a good deal.

THE HEADRIGHT SYSTEM

Indentured servants were not the only people who gained land under this business model. The landowners for whom the indentured servants worked did, too. Under what was called the headright system, for each servant the landowner brought to North America, the landowner received 50 acres (20 ha) of land. In this way, the landowner was able to increase their property holdings and receive the services of the indentured servant for the term of the contract. Additionally, the colony itself grew in strength and power as its landowners amassed more land.

HOW IT WORKED

The people who agreed to this plan were known as indentured servants. Most of them were skilled or unskilled laborers who had difficulty finding work in Europe. The Thirty Years' War had recently ended, leaving behind an economic depression. There were no longer enough jobs to go around.

After arriving in North America, indentured servants would work for their new master for four to seven years. In return, their master paid for their passage to the Americas and also provided room and board, but the servants were not paid for their work. At the end of the contract came the freedom dues, such as land, money, food, clothes, or weapons. The length of the required contract could be extended if the servant broke any sort of law, or if a female servant became pregnant.

Fallout from the Thirty Years' War sent many Europeans to North America in search of a better life.

A HARSH LIFE

It sounds a lot like slavery, and in a way it was. The conditions were relatively harsh, and indentured servants had a lot of restrictions placed on them. They were required to be faithful, meek, and obedient to the landowner. There were laws to punish indentured servants who attempted to run away, or those who attempted to hire themselves out to other landowners under better terms.

There were also strict rules forbidding relationships between indentured servants. Female indentured servants faced particularly harsh punishment under such laws. If they were to become pregnant with a child by the landowner, the female servant would be sold to the local church parish for two years after completing her contract.

»» ELIZABETH ABBOTT AND ELIAS HINTON

VICTIMS OF INVOLUNTARY SERVITUDE

Elizabeth Abbott, a young beggar woman, came to Virginia as an indentured servant in 1618. She served in the house of John and Alice Proctor, where she was often beaten for running away and other offenses. In one such beating she was reportedly lashed 500 times. Eventually, Alice Proctor inflicted a fatal beating on Abbott using a thick cord studded with fishhooks. The General Court of Colonial Virginia reported that her body was found wrapped in a rug behind a boat. Above the waist, her body was covered with open sores.

The Proctors had another indentured servant, Elias Hinton, who worked in the Proctors' tobacco fields. Hinton was beaten by both Alice and John Proctor, and he was ultimately beaten to death with a rake.

WORKING HARD

The living conditions were harsh for indentured servants. In Virginia, workers in the tobacco fields toiled for six days a week, from sunup to sundown, from February through November. Their living conditions were primitive and often unsanitary. If they became sick, they were still forced to work in the fields. Many of them died as a result.

However, in many ways indentured servitude differed from slavery. Indentured servants came over of their own choice, lured by the promise of a better life. Additionally, they had the promise of eventual freedom and land ownership, as long as they fulfilled the terms of their contract. They also had laws to protect some of their rights, unlike slaves.

BETTER THAN SLAVERY?

The life of an indentured servant was far from easy, but it was much more promising than the life of a slave. It is estimated that half to two-thirds of all immigrants who came to the colonies did so as indentured servants. While most of them enjoyed a simple, modest life once they fulfilled their contract, some eventually became members of the colonial elite. Unfortunately, a large percentage of indentured servants did not live long enough to fulfill their contract and gain their full freedom as citizens of America. Historians estimate that about 60 percent died before they could fulfill their contract.

SLAVERY IN THE COLONIES

Slavery actually started much like indentured servitude. There were no slave laws governing the treatment or rights of slaves when the first Africans arrived in Virginia in 1619, so white landowners tended to treat them similarly to how they treated European indentured servants. However, in the following few decades, that began to change.

A NEW SYSTEM

White landowners were becoming increasingly frustrated by the concept of indentured servitude. The indentured servants were fulfilling their contracts and becoming eligible to receive land, which some landowners perceived as a threat. Additionally, indentured servants were starting to band together to fight against poor treatment, much to the landowners' dismay. The landowners eventually decided that slavery was a more profitable labor system, since the slaves had no chance of fulfilling a contract and demanding land in return. There were also laws establishing slaves' rights (or lack thereof). Essentially, they were cheap labor that made no demands, and so slaves became more desirable than indentured servants.

Slaves often did the same work as indentured servants, but landowners did not have to allow them any of the few freedoms that indentured servants had.

BACON'S REBELLION

One of the first displays of unrest among indentured servants was Bacon's Rebellion, which occurred in Jamestown in 1676. Nathaniel Bacon was from a wealthy English family and had settled in Jamestown after his father paid his passage across the Atlantic. Native Americans had been responsible for a series of attacks on frontier settlements, and Governor William Berkeley refused to retaliate.

Bacon's anger at the governor's refusal to take action led him to mount a rebellion. The rebellion was only partly successful. King Charles II stripped Berkeley of his governorship after the rebellion, but the rebels did not succeed in their goal of driving Native Americans out of the region.

What makes the rebellion notable is that it caused indentured servants and slaves to join together in an alliance against the ruling class. It was a wake-up call for the wealthy landowners that indentured servants were becoming increasingly discontented. Obviously slaves wanted change as well, but they did not have the same rights as indentured servants, so it was easier for landowners to keep them under control.

Bacon's Rebellion marked a turning point in the relationship between indentured servants and landowners.

SLAVERY IN THE SOUTH

During the colonial era, slaves were brought to North America to work in many regions, though many were in the South. The economy in the southern regions revolved around farming, an industry in which it was easy to integrate slave labor. Slaves quickly became an integral part of the economy of the South, performing the backbreaking labor needed on tobacco, rice, and indigo plantations. The economy in the northern states tended not to require slave labor, so there was less slave ownership in the North.

AFTER THE AMERICAN REVOLUTION

Once the United States was formed, it was no longer under English rule, but a divide soon began to show up between the North and the South. The South was a strongly slave-holding region, while the North was not, and northerners began to question the use of slaves in the South. Northerners saw slavery as not so very different from what colonists had suffered while under British rule. The harsh conditions were different, certainly, but much like the slaves did not have freedom, the first colonists had been forced to live under British rule, which did not seem all that much like freedom either.

COLONIAL SLAVERY BY THE NUMBERS

In the period leading up to the American Revolution, slaves came to the colonies from Africa by the thousands. In Virginia, where slaves were brought in to work in the tobacco fields, historians estimate that around 2,000 slaves were imported each decade from the 1670s through the 1690s. From the 1700s to the 1750s, Virginia imported between 12,000 and 28,000 slaves per decade.

South Carolina was rice-growing country, and between 1701 and 1720, 2,500 slaves were imported. However, from the 1720s to the 1740s, approximately 35,000 slaves were brought to South Carolina. From the 1750s to the 1790s, the number was between 22,000 and 28,000 slaves per decade.

The practice of importing slaves was so common that by the U.S. Census in 1790, people of African descent made up nearly 18 percent of the American population. In total, it is estimated that between 1525 and 1866, approximately 388,000 slaves were brought to the colonies that became the United States.

Slaves were an integral part of the Southern economy in the 18th century.

THE CIVIL WAR

The Northern states slowly began to turn against slavery, and by 1804 it had been abolished in all Northern states. In 1808, the Act Prohibiting Importation of Slaves went into effect, stating that no new slaves could be brought into the United States, either in the North or the South. However, slave trade was still allowed within the states, so the act did not mark the end of slavery.

The abolitionist movement began in the 1830s and lasted for about three decades, until the end of the Civil War. The Civil War was the result of tensions between the North and South, primarily over slavery. Many Southern states seceded from the Union and formed a new country that they called the Confederate States of America. A bloody war followed, which the Confederacy lost in 1865.

THE END OF SLAVERY

Two years before the war's end, President Abraham Lincoln had signed the Emancipation Proclamation. This document granted freedom to slaves in areas rebelling against the government. It could not be enforced in Confederate regions, but slaves escaping those areas immediately became free.

With the passage of the 13th Amendment to the Constitution in 1865, slavery was fully outlawed in all the United States, and slaves earned the right to pursue citizenship. The Civil Rights Act of 1866 declared that children born to immigrant slaves were automatically granted United States citizenship.

The Emancipation Proclamation—shown here being read to Lincoln's cabinet—was a major step toward ending slavery.

23

CHAPTER 3

NINETEENTH-CENTURY IMMIGRATION

The United States has experienced a number of waves of immigration, starting even before it was officially the United States. There was a large wave of European and slave immigrants during the colonial era, with people coming over to the "New World" in hopes of a better life—or, in the case of slaves, because they were forced into labor.

After an initial wave of immigration during the colonial era, the United States experienced a bit of a slowdown in the late 18th and early 19th centuries. Part of this slowdown was likely due to the fact that in 1808, the Act Prohibiting Importation of Slaves went into effect, which made it illegal for landowners and investors to import slaves into America.

However, starting in 1815, the next big wave of immigration began, and over the next 50 years, it brought in millions of immigrants from northern and western Europe. Another wave began in the 1880s.

IRISH IMMIGRATION

Many of the immigrants who came over in the first half of the 19th century were from Ireland. At that time Ireland was heavily dependent on potato farming, and a disease called potato blight destroyed potato crops in the 1840s. It resulted in mass starvation and disease across Ireland from 1845 to 1849. More than 1 million people died, and of those who did not, another million left Ireland, with many immigrating to the United States.

Irish families often could not afford to immigrate to the United States together, so one member of the family would go to the United States, find work, and send money back to the family in Ireland. As funds allowed, further members of the family would then come to the United States.

Irish people fleeing the Potato Famine were often blessed by priests before embarking on their long journey.

A POOR RECEPTION

The Irish who came to America typically did not have much money. The Potato Famine, among other factors, had left them with little. Because they could not afford onward travel, they tended to settle in the port cities where they docked when they arrived—such as Boston, New York City, and Baltimore. Many settled in Philadelphia as well, which was reasonably accessible from New York City and other nearby ports.

The Irish were essentially the first poor refugees to arrive in America, and they were not always welcomed. Jobs were hard to come by, and natural-born Americans or those who had immigrated with more money tended to look down on the Irish immigrants.

The British government tried to help the starving Irish during the Potato Famine, but many people felt that they did not do enough.

IMMIGRANT LIFE

Life for Irish immigrants was particularly tough in Boston. Boston had begun as a Puritan colony, and many of its elite were descended from the original colonists. The Irish immigrants were generally Catholic, who did not necessarily get along with the Protestant Bostonians. The wealthy elite in Boston scorned the Irish immigrants because they were poor and often unskilled.

There was a huge demand for housing, particularly in 1847, when a reported 37,000 Irish immigrants arrived in Boston. Landlords in Boston took advantage of this, and many rented rooms to Irish immigrants for high prices—despite the rooms having no water, sanitation, or ventilation. Some immigrants ended up living in backyards and alleys, in wooden shacks. Others lived in cellars that frequently flooded and were perpetually damp and musty.

HEALTH AND DISEASE

These conditions were a recipe for disaster. The average Irish immigrant lived only six years after arriving in Boston, due in large part to the poor living conditions. About 60 percent of children born to Irish immigrant families in Boston during this time died by the age of 5.

Disease was not the only issue, either. Living in such deplorable conditions, Irish immigrants faced despair. The Boston Committee of Internal Health called the Irish slums "a perfect hive of human beings, without comforts and mostly without common necessaries; in many cases huddled together like brutes… Under such circumstances… sullen indifference and despair or disorder, intemperance and utter degradation reign supreme."

THE IRISH IN NEW YORK

New York City was an even more popular landing spot for Irish immigrants. Historians estimate that about 75 percent of the Irish immigrants who came to the United States as a result of the Potato Famine ended up in New York City. Because it was a much bigger city than Boston, in some ways New York City was better able to support the huge influx of immigrants.

Life in New York City still was not easy for incoming Irish immigrants. Fellow Irish who had been in the States longer, called "runners," would meet them at the docks and offer to help them find a place to stay. However, the offer was not really genuine—the runners would set immigrants up in filthy boarding houses at higher rates than promised. When the immigrants' money ran out, their luggage would be confiscated and they would end up on the streets.

Many immigrants heading to New York left from Queenstown, a major Irish port.

RUNNERS

Runners did not only prey on Irish immigrants. New York City had a diverse population, and for each nationality of immigrant, there were runners eagerly waiting to take advantage of the newcomers. English runners preyed on English immigrants, and German runners preyed on German immigrants.

Once a ship docked at Staten Island, an 1850s newspaper wrote, "a gang of 300 or 400 ruffians calling themselves runners would jump aboard and in the style of plunderers, or pirates seize all of the baggage and endeavor to persuade passengers to such and such lodging house."

Other scams used by runners involved selling immigrants fake railroad and boat tickets, for those who wanted to go someplace other than New York. Sometimes the tickets were utterly worthless, and other times they were valid but the immigrant was forced into a steerage section and threatened with being thrown overboard if he did not pay more money.

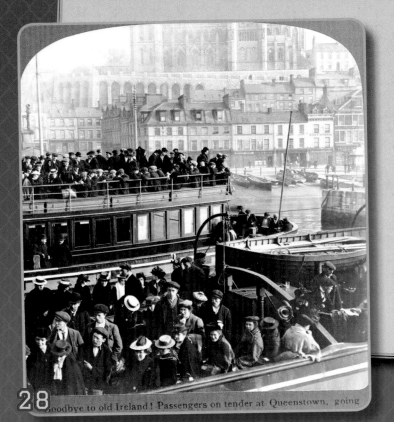

Goodbye to old Ireland! Passengers on tender at Queenstown, going

The luckiest immigrants managed to avoid dealing with runners once they arrived in the United States.

Immigration from Germany

Another significant number of immigrants during this period came from Germany. In the 1840s, the country was facing economic problems and growing unemployment. This led the lower classes to revolt against the government in 1848.

The revolution was essentially a political struggle between liberals and conservatives. The middle and working classes generally made up the liberals. They wanted a more democratic government and guaranteed human rights. On the other hand, the aristocracy was conservative, wanting to keep things the way they were. The middle and working classes eventually split in their ideals, which allowed the conservative aristocracy to win.

Many people fled the country to escape from the fighting and from the revolution's aftermath. For the working classes, the prospects in Germany were rather bleak after the revolution of 1848. Moving to the United States offered the possibility of a better life.

Chain migration

From 1830 until the outbreak of World War I in 1914, nearly 90 percent of the people who left Germany came to the United States. By 1832, more than 10,000 German immigrants had arrived in the United States. These immigrants would then write to their families and friends back in Germany, describing their new life in America. Their letters would prompt a chain migration in which more German immigrants would arrive. By 1854, almost 200,000 German immigrants had come to the United States.

German immigration to the United States remained high throughout much of the 19th century.

FLEEING PERSECUTION

When the liberals failed to reform the German government, many fled to the United States to avoid persecution. Before the revolution, they had faced unemployment and land seizures. As government opponents in the revolution —part of the losing side—they then faced political persecution. More than 5 million German citizens ultimately immigrated to the United States.

Around the same time, anti-Semitism was beginning to grow in Germany. Many Jews no longer felt safe in Germany and fled to the United States in search of religious freedom. These immigrants made a much smaller group than those fleeing the revolution, but even so, nearly 15,000 European Jews had immigrated to the United States by the middle of the 19th century. Given the anti-Semitism and persecution of Jews that would happen in the following century, it was probably a very wise decision.

JOSEPH PULITZER

FAMOUS FACES

Although Germany and Ireland were the main sources of immigrants in the mid-19th century, people came from other countries as well. One such immigrant was a young man named Joseph Pulitzer, a Hungarian Jew who immigrated to Boston in 1864 at the age of 17.

The military in the North needed more soldiers to fight in the Civil War, so they offered to pay their passage from overseas. Pulitzer's family had been living in poverty since his father's death, so he took advantage of the opportunity. After the war, Pulitzer became a well-known newspaper publisher, and the coveted Pulitzer Prize that bears his name was created by Columbia University in 1917.

THE GOLD RUSH

Around the same time, another event drew immigrants to the United States: the Gold Rush. Gold was discovered in the American River in northern California on January 24, 1848. Gold was incredibly valuable, so when news of this discovery spread, it brought a huge influx of people to the area to search for gold. These prospectors were often called the 49ers, since many arrived in 1849.

Some of the prospectors who came in search of riches were from the eastern United States—already U.S. citizens. However, others came from Europe (Germany, France, and Ireland), Mexico and South America, Turkey, and China. The population growth was particularly strong in the port city of San Francisco. In 1848 it had a population of just 1,000 people, but by 1850 it had grown to more than 20,000.

The 49ers sought their fortune in northern California's mountains and streams, but few ever struck it rich.

CHINESE IMMIGRANTS

A large number of immigrants from China arrived during the Gold Rush, and Americans tended to be quite suspicious of them. Xenophobia was common, and Chinese immigrants were very different from the people most American citizens were familiar with. They looked different to Europeans, and their language—based on a whole different alphabet—sounded strange to American ears. Their customs seemed entirely foreign, causing mistrust.

It made for a tense time. On the West Coast, between 1848 and 1852, the Chinese immigrant population grew from 400 people to 20,000 people. The population explosion did not make white Americans any more open to the Chinese immigrants, either. Some Chinese immigrants were murdered, and organizations hoping to ban Asian immigration were formed.

 The Gold Rush drew many Chinese immigrants, before new laws limited—and eventually banned—their immigration.

EUROPEAN MIGRATION BY THE NUMBERS

Many Chinese immigrants came to prospect or work in the gold mines, but many ended up working in another profession entirely: building the transcontinental railroad. Railroad work was backbreaking labor, and contractor Charles Crocker had trouble maintaining a good crew of workers.

Before the Chinese arrived, the railroads had used mostly Irish immigrants. Whether it was justified or not, the Irish had the reputation of being lazy workers who spent all their money on liquor and frequently got into fights. So Crocker decided to try hiring Chinese immigrants instead, even though most people claimed they were equally unreliable.

Crocker found that the Chinese he hired had an outstanding work ethic. "Wherever we put them, we found them good, and they worked themselves into our favor to such an extent that if we found we were in a hurry for a job of work, it was better to put Chinese on at once." By 1868, 80 percent of the Central Pacific Railroad workforce was made up of Chinese laborers.

IMMIGRATION BANS

The government was not on the side of Chinese and other Asian immigrants. In 1875 they passed the Page Act, which barred Asian immigrants from coming to the United States for jobs in forced labor. The act also succeeded in barring most Chinese women from coming to the United States, as it was suspected they were coming to work as prostitutes.

In 1882, Congress prohibited nearly all immigration from China when it passed the Chinese Exclusion Act. Immigration for Chinese citizens did not really open up again until 1943, when the Magnuson Act allowed a quota of just 105 Chinese citizens to immigrate per year.

CHAPTER 4

IMMIGRATION FROM 1900 TO 1950

Another wave of European immigration occurred between 1880 and 1920. Many of the estimated 20 million immigrants in that period came from Central, Eastern, and Southern Europe. More than 2 million of those were Jews from Eastern Europe, fleeing religious persecution, and about 600,000 were from Italy.

NEW LEGISLATION

Although many of them came from immigrant stock themselves, some Americans began to worry about the impact of such large numbers of immigrants on their society and economy. In response to this, Congress passed the Immigration Act of 1903. Among other things, it banned several categories of people from entering the country, including anarchists, epileptics, beggars, and importers of prostitutes.

Jews fled to the United States to avoid persecution and ended up settling neighborhoods with markets and stores.

Four years later, Congress passed the Immigration Act of 1907, which put further restrictions on who could enter the country. Specifically, the law stipulated that people with various types of disabilities would not be admitted to the country. It listed all the reasons that a person could be barred from entering:

> All idiots, imbeciles, feebleminded persons, epileptics, insane persons, and persons who have been insane within five years previous; persons who have had two or more attacks of insanity at any time previously; paupers; persons likely to become a public charge; professional beggars; persons afflicted with tuberculosis or with a loathsome or dangerous contagious disease; persons not comprehended within any of the foregoing excluded classes who are found to be and are certified by the examining surgeon as being mentally or physically defective, such mental or physical defect being of a nature which may affect the ability of such alien to earn a living.

SETTING LIMITS

The Immigration Act of 1907 successfully denied entry to people with any sort of disability or illness that might make it difficult for them to earn a living. A Presidential Coalition was soon formed to study the causes and effects of the mass immigration to the United States from Europe. The results of that study informed the writing of a new law.

The Immigration Act of 1917 made sweeping changes to immigration laws in the United States. Specifically, it required all immigrants over the age of 16 to pass a literacy test. It also banned homosexual immigrants from entering the country, as well as people from most Asian countries.

Immigrants had to pass a physical exam before they were allowed into the United States.

ELLIS ISLAND

One of the most famous entry points for immigrants was Ellis Island, near the Statue of Liberty. It was turned into a federal immigration station in 1892 by President Benjamin Harrison. Until 1954, immigrants arriving by ship to New York City checked in at Ellis Island. During its 62 years of operation, Ellis Island welcomed more than 12 million immigrants.

Ellis Island became a symbol of the masses who immigrated to the United States, looking for a better life.

WORLD WAR I

World War I began in Europe in 1914. In the years leading up to it, many immigrants came to the United States, fleeing religious persecution and growing political strife. Americans feared these immigrants would bring undesirable ideas with them.

There were hundreds of thousands of German immigrants in the country. Although the United States stayed out of the war until 1917, many people sympathized with the countries fighting against Germany. They became suspicious of German-American citizens, thinking that they would side with Germany instead of the United States when war came.

When a German submarine torpedoed the passenger ship *Lusitania*, killing 128 Americans, anti-German sentiment grew even stronger. Many German-Americans changed their names and altered their customs so as not to be identified as Germans.

SETTING QUOTAS

During this period, many Americans were also concerned about allowing anarchists, Jews, and Bolsheviks into the country. In response to these fears, Congress passed the Emergency Quota Act in 1921, which was intended to limit the number of immigrants to the United States. It did this by establishing quotas for how many people of any given nationality would be allowed entry.

Some immigrants who were denied entry were detained at Ellis Island while waiting to be sent back home. »

IMMIGRATION AFTER WORLD WAR I

As a follow-up to the Emergency Quota Act in 1921, Congress passed the Immigration Act of 1924, also known as the Johnson-Reed Act. The Emergency Quota Act had limited the number of immigrants from any given country to 3 percent of the total number of people from that country who were already living in the United States. The Immigration Act of 1924 lowered that quota to 2 percent.

The act also used the 1890 United States Census as its basis, instead of the 1910 census that the Emergency Quota Act had used. This further limited the number of immigrants, because the total number of U.S. residents from a given country was obviously lower in the 1890 census, taken before the mass influx of immigrants into the United States between 1890 and 1910.

EFFECTS OF THE ACT

The Immigration Act of 1924 was not just concerned with limiting immigration from Europe. It also established strong restrictions of the number of African immigrants allowed into the country. It completely banned immigration of Arabs and people from Asia.

Until very recently, it was hard to imagine Congress passing laws that outright forbid the immigration of certain groups of people. However, the 1920s was a period of post-war unease. People still had concerns about Germany and the other competing forces that led up to World War I. By citing national security, Congress was able to pass laws that today seem surprisingly restrictive.

A UNITED NATION?

According to the United States Office of the Historian, the purpose of the Immigration Act of 1924 was to "preserve the ideal of U.S. homogeneity," which was what most people wanted. Many Americans were okay with the idea of their country being a "melting pot"—as long as the cultures all melted together into one homogenous American culture. They were suspicious of immigrants who kept their customs, language, and traditions even after moving to the United States.

SLOWING DOWN

The Immigration Act of 1924, combined with other restrictions, led to a 40-year slowdown in immigration. Events such as the Great Depression, World War II, and the Cold War also contributed to the slowdown. The promise of a new life in America did not seem so sweet when the nation was plunged into a 10-year economic downturn, with jobs scarce and people starving.

Also, the United States was not the only nation hit by the Depression. Its effects were felt around the world, including in countries such as Germany and the United Kingdom. Even if people had wanted to come to the United States, could they have afforded to during a depression? With strict immigration quotas in place, they were unable to.

Immigration to the United States slowed during the Great Depression, when jobs were scarce and poverty was widespread.

IMMIGRATION AND WORLD WAR II

In fact, the economic depression is part of what allowed Adolf Hitler to rise to power in Germany, ultimately sparking World War II and a fresh wave of anti-German sentiment. German citizens were distraught at the conditions in their country after losing World War I, and Hitler promised a new and prosperous future. He gained popularity and power, and by the time people recognized the danger of his Nazi Party, he already had immense control over the nation.

FLEEING GERMANY

Jews and others who did not fit Hitler's idea of a master race needed to flee Germany, but they were running out of places to go. Hitler was steadily and systematically taking control of other European countries, so the safest option was for refugees to leave Europe entirely.

However, in the early 1940s, America was not a good option for these refugees. The American government was afraid of Nazi spies and saboteurs entering the country. Immigrants fleeing persecution were screened incredibly heavily and often not allowed into the country. The situation improved in 1944, when President Franklin Delano Roosevelt established the War Refugee Board. This organization helped to rescue thousands of Jews from Hungary, Romania, and other European countries.

 After the attack on Pearl Harbor, Japanese were seen as the enemy—even those with American citizenship, like this store owner of Japanese ancestry.

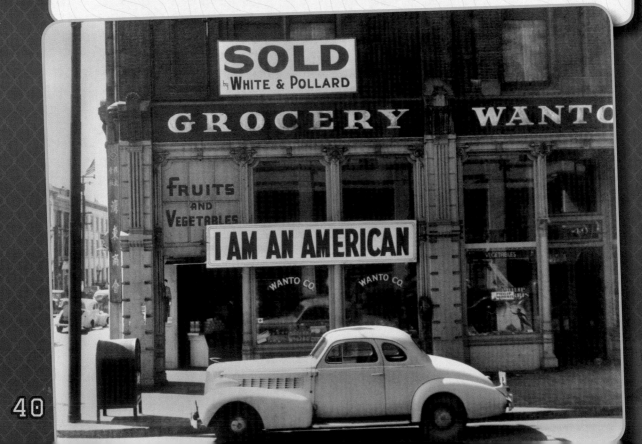

EVA SCHOTT

Eighteen-year-old Eva Schott was one of the few German Jews to be allowed entry to the United States during the war. She was lucky—some family members lived in the United States and had sponsored Eva's family for a visa. However, the journey to America was not a simple one. Germany would not allow people to emigrate through Europe, so the Schotts had to travel through the Baltic states into the Soviet Union, then through China to Japan, before sailing across the Pacific Ocean to the United States.

After three weeks on the ship, they arrived in San Francisco, where Eva and her mother were placed in the Angel Island Immigration Station Hospital, while her father was detained elsewhere on the island. They were questioned extensively, until the authorities were sufficiently convinced that they were not spies and that they would be able to provide for themselves.

AFTER THE WAR

When the war ended in 1945 with the fall of Hitler, thousands of Jews were released from concentration camps. These so-called displaced persons often did not have homes or families to return to. Not surprisingly, many of them left Europe entirely to escape anti-Semitism and Communism.

Many of the displaced persons fled to Palestine, and nearly as many headed for the United States. Immigration restrictions were still in place in the United States, but suddenly the nation was faced with an influx of tens of thousands of displaced persons. To accommodate this, President Harry Truman issued the Truman Directive in late 1945, which granted visas to the displaced immigrants—but only within existing quotas. As a result, more than 22,000 displaced European refugees entered the United States between 1945 and 1947.

NEW QUOTAS

However, those 22,000 immigrants represented only a fraction of the displaced persons needing a new home. The Jewish community in America lobbied heavily for legislation to allow more Jewish displaced persons to enter America, and in response Congress passed the Displaced Persons Act of 1948. It allowed 200,000 displaced persons to enter the United States. Nearly 80,000 were Jewish, and the rest were residents of Eastern Europe and the Baltic states who had been forced into labor by Germany.

President Truman felt that the 1948 legislation discriminated against Jews, and Congress amended the law in 1950. Although most Jewish immigrants turned away from the United States had settled in Israel by then, the legislation enacted in 1948 and amended in 1950 established a precedent for immigration during future refugee crises.

IMMIGRATION AND NATIONALITY ACT OF 1952

Another important piece of legislation was the Immigration and Nationality Act of 1952, also known as the McCarran-Walter Act. It was an incredibly controversial piece of legislation, because many people thought it was discriminatory.

Basically, the act established a preference system for immigrants. People who wanted to come to the United States were divided into several basic groups: immigrants with special skills, relatives of U.S. citizens who were exempt from quotas, average immigrants who were subject to quotas, and refugees. Whether they were allowed admittance to the United States depended partly on which group they fell under.

In practice, the act allowed officials to discriminate against people from ethnic groups and nationalities considered as not desirable. Immigrants could also be banned from entering the country based on political beliefs.

TRUMAN'S VETO

President Harry Truman vetoed the bill on June 25, 1952, but his veto was overridden by both the House and Senate in the following days, and the act passed into law. In his veto, Truman stated that some of the bill's provisions met with his approval, but others did not. He agreed that United States laws regarding immigration needed to be revised and updated, but he felt the McCarran-Walter Act did not provide an adequate policy. He wrote:

> The bill...would be a step backward and not a step forward ... It is incredible to me that, in this year of 1952, we should again be enacting into law such a slur on the patriotism, the capacity, and the decency of a large part of our citizenry.

President Harry Truman tried to veto the Immigration and Nationality Act of 1952 because he thought it was discriminatory.

EDMONSTON STUDIO

CHAPTER 5
IMMIGRATION 1950S TO PRESENT

The 1950s was a rather tense time in United States history. The Cold War was underway, with U.S. involvement in a proxy war in Korea. Senator Joseph McCarthy helped fuel Americans' fear of communism with his blacklist of suspected Communists. In short, there was still significant unease about immigrants entering and living in the United States.

ON THE BLACKLIST

In the era of McCarthyism, numerous celebrities were singled out as possible Communist Party sympathizers and banned from working in the entertainment industry. Acclaimed screenwriter Dalton Trumbo was one of the first to make the blacklist. Other well-known celebrities on the list included playwright Lillian Hellman, singer Lena Horne, singer Burl Ives, playwright Arthur Miller, director Orson Welles, actress Katharine Hepburn, and actor Humphrey Bogart.

FAMOUS FACES

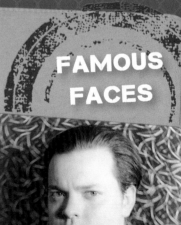

Film director Orson Welles was included on the McCarthy blacklist.

Cuban Immigration

One perceived threat close to U.S. soil was Cuba. Just 90 miles (144.8 km) off the coast of Florida, Cuba's political situation was tense. Fulgencio Batista had assumed the presidency of Cuba in 1952, under what many considered a dictatorship. Batista cut Cuba's ties with the Soviet Union and persecuted Cuban socialists. This led Fidel Castro to form a revolutionary group that ultimately overthrew Batista's rule in 1959. Shortly after installing himself as leader of Cuba, Castro reestablished Cuban ties with the Soviet Union—the United States' opponent in the Cold War.

Cuban leader Fidel Castro was seen by many in the United States as an enemy because of his Communist beliefs.

Castro's takeover of the Cuban government led a refugee crisis to arise around 1960. Reacting to Castro's Communist policies and his ties to the Soviet Union, hundreds of thousands of Cubans fled the nation between 1960 and 1979. In the first years, more than 14,000 Cuban children were sent to the United States, while their parents remained in Cuba. Some of these children went to live with relatives already settled in the United States. Others went into foster homes or orphanages, or sometimes to boarding schools.

The Cuban Adjustment Act

To accommodate the influx of immigrants from Cuba, Congress under President Lyndon B. Johnson passed the Cuban Adjustment Act in 1966. This legislation made immigration from Cuba much simpler. It stated that Cubans who feared persecution in Cuba could apply to come to the United States as refugees. It also made Cubans exempt from immigration quotas as well as some of the requirements faced by other immigrants.

IMMIGRATION AND NATIONALITY ACT OF 1965

The civil rights movement started around 1954 and continued throughout the 1960s. Much of it was focused on abolishing discrimination based on race, color, religion, gender, or nationality. Several important pieces of legislation were passed during this era, but the most relevant to immigrants was the Immigration and Nationality Act of 1965.

 The civil rights movement helped start breaking down the divide between black and white citizens.

The act was based on the findings of the Commission on Immigration and Naturalization. Under a 1952 order from President Harry Truman, they had conducted an investigation into immigration regulations. Truman had been strongly against the discriminatory quota practices of immigration laws in the 1950s. During the civil rights movement in the 1960s, the new president, John F. Kennedy, felt the same. In a speech to the American Committee on Italian Migration in 1963, he said:

"There are still a good many brothers and sisters of American citizens who are unable to get here, who may have preferences as members of families but because of the maldistribution of quotas in the European area we have this situation which has become nearly intolerable, where you have thousands of unused quotas in some countries while you have members of families, close members of families, in other countries who are desirous of coming to this country, who can become useful citizens, whose skills are needed, who are unable to come because of the inequity and the maldistribution of the quota numbers."

 President John F. Kennedy met with civil rights leaders, including Martin Luther King, Jr., in Washington in 1963.

EFFECTS OF THE ACT

The bill took a couple more years to pass, but ultimately, it was signed into law by President Lyndon Johnson in 1965. It abolished the practice of using race, ancestry, or national origin as criteria for determining immigration eligibility. No longer could someone be denied entry into the United States simply because they were from Africa or Asia, and immediate family of United States citizens were no longer subject to immigration quotas and were given immigration priority.

The Immigration and Nationality Act of 1965 was a big step forward in getting rid of discriminatory practices based on nationality, but there was one area where immigration laws still allowed outright discrimination. Under this act, Immigration Services could reject homosexual immigrants because they were seen as "mentally defective" or with a "psychopathic inferiority." It was not until 1990 that discriminatory immigration laws against homosexuals were barred.

IMMIGRATION AND ECONOMICS

In the late 1970s and early 1980s, the United States experienced high unemployment, high inflation, and an economic recession. It was not as bad as the economic devastation they had experienced during the Great Depression in the 1930s. Even so, the high rates of unemployment and the economic slump were enough to be troubling.

Some people felt one reason for the high rates of unemployment was the practice of hiring undocumented immigrants, often referred to as illegal or unauthorized aliens. These undocumented immigrants would often work for lower wages than American citizens. In some cases they were paid "under the table," which meant employers did not put them on an official payroll. This meant that they did not pay Social Security and other taxes for the undocumented workers. This practice was illegal, but many employers felt that the money they saved was worth the risk of penalties or prosecution.

 ## WHY HIRE UNDOCUMENTED WORKERS?

Some people wonder why an employer would hire an undocumented immigrant over an American citizen. One East Coast landscaper who has hired approximately 50 undocumented immigrants from Mexico explained why, although he insisted on remaining anonymous, since admitting what he did could lead to penalty or prosecution.

The landscaper has hired—and continues to hire—American citizens. However, he often found them unreliable or unwilling to do the landscaping work. Many have quit, and he has had to fire others. In contrast, the undocumented Mexican workers he has hired are eager for as many hours as he will give them and are often willing to work seven days a week. These workers are desperate for money to send back to their families in Mexico, and the landscaper pays them the same as he pays his American employees—well above minimum wage.

Mexican laborers—both documented and undocumented—make up a major part of the workforce on California's farms.

The landscaper commented that one worker makes $25, which is more than double minimum wage.

It is a questionable practice—but one with motivations that go deeper than one might think. It is not about the landscaper hiring Mexican laborers because they work for little money; it is about him hiring them because they are willing to do the work. As for the Mexican laborers, they are happy for decent pay to send home to their families.

CRACKING DOWN

The Immigration Reform and Control Act was enacted in 1986. The idea behind it was to make it more difficult for employers to use undocumented immigrants as part of their workforce. The act made it illegal to knowingly hire or recruit undocumented immigrants, except for certain undocumented immigrants used for seasonal agricultural work. It also required employers to attest to all of their employees' immigration status. The act did not have much effect on the number of undocumented immigrants living in the United States, but it did provide some stricter guidelines for future hiring practices.

The act also legalized immigrants who had resided in the United States continuously since January 1, 1982, and who could prove they were not guilty of a crime. These immigrants also had to show that they had a basic knowledge of U.S. history, government, and the English language. These immigrants had to pay a fine and any back taxes due, and they had to admit they had resided in the United States illegally. Still, for many of them, it was a chance for citizenship.

THE IMMIGRATION ACT OF 1990

In 1990, Senator Ted Kennedy proposed a reform of the Immigration and Nationality Act of 1965. The new bill, known as the Immigration Act of 1990, was signed into law by President George H.W. Bush. It increased the total number of immigrants allowed into the United States each year, and it lifted the ban on homosexuals entering the United States. It also created new types of visas under which immigrants could enter the United States.

Temporary protected status

One such visa that was introduced was the temporary protected status (TPS) visa, which allowed refugees to remain in the United States when it was unsafe for them to return to their home country. The TPS visa was a major change to immigration policy. Under it, citizens from unsafe countries could remain in the United States until their TPS status was withdrawn.

TPS is not the same thing as a green card, which can ultimately lead to citizenship, but it does provide some protection for citizens from countries that have been devastated by natural disaster or are unsafe because of unstable political conditions. For example, citizens of Haiti, El Salvador, and Nepal can apply for a TPS visa based on devastating earthquakes. And citizens of Somalia, Sudan, South Sudan, and Yemen are eligible due to political conflict and instability.

The TPS visa was designed to help victims of natural disasters, such as these survivors of the earthquake that hit Nepal in 2015.

THE TECH BOOM

The 1970s, when the first personal computers were developed, saw the beginning of a technology boom. Ever since then, the technology sector has been in a mad race to see who can develop the fastest, most exciting new applications and software to run on the best-designed new hardware.

This boom has meant job growth, and many of those tech jobs have been filled by immigrant workers. Some companies establish offshore outlets in countries where wages are lower, such as India. Others simply arrange visas to bring in workers from other countries. In the United States, about 24 percent of tech jobs are held by immigrants.

Technology workers are just some of the many immigrants to come to the United States under work visas.

H-1B VERSUS EB-1

Most immigrants who come to the United States to work in the tech field come under an H-1B visa. With this type of visa, a United States employer has offered a job to a potential immigrant and intends for that person to have continued employment with the company.

Other immigrants enter the country under an EB-1 visa. "EB" stands for "employment based," and the immigrant has to be able to prove that they have extraordinary ability in some certain field. Often this is reserved for people in the arts, but it can also be applied to technology fields.

Skilled immigrants

Some people worry that hiring immigrants for jobs at American companies leads to fewer jobs being available for American citizens. However, professors from Harvard Business School, Wellesley College, and Johns Hopkins University disagree. They published their research in a 2013 publication.

In their analysis of 319 U.S. firms, the professors found that hiring immigrants actually increased their hiring of U.S. workers, too. Microsoft founder Bill Gates, for example, said that for every one immigrant his company hires under the H-1B visa, Microsoft hires four additional American workers.

Microsoft founder Bill Gates has spoken to Congress about the need for highly educated foreign workers.

The study also found that immigrant workers were not pushing older U.S. employees out of jobs, as some thought. Some employers revealed that they hire tech labor from overseas because that is where the workers are available—there are not enough tech graduates coming out of American universities to fill the jobs.

Looking Forward

The debate remains about whether hiring immigrant workers is benefiting the U.S. economy or taking away jobs from citizens. In fact, it was one of the hotly debated topics in the 2016 presidential election.

CHAPTER 6

IMMIGRATION TODAY

Immigration was a hot topic in the 2016 presidential election, and today's immigration laws are a far cry from those established when the country was founded. As the makeup of the nation and the world shifts, no doubt immigration policies will continue to change. However, for the moment, it is useful to understand the current immigration laws governing the United States.

CURRENT IMMIGRATION LAWS

United States immigration policy has four main goals: welcoming immigrants with skills that will benefit the economy, reuniting families, promoting diversity, and protecting refugees. The laws on immigration are complex, but there are some general rules and standards used. For example, the current annual limit of immigrants allowed in the United States is 675,000. However, there are exceptions made when it is a case of a close family member joining one already living in the United States.

When an immigrant enters the country, they can apply for a green card if they wish to live and work permanently in the United States. If their application is approved, the green card will also allow them to eventually apply for naturalization and the benefits and rights of full citizenship, if they choose.

In addition, in some circumstances the government allows noncitizens to come into the country on a temporary basis. These rules apply to students seeking an education at a U.S. university. There are also a certain number of refugees allowed in each year.

Employment-based immigration

Immigrants coming to work in the United States can either get a temporary visa or apply for a green card. Only 140,000 of these immigrants can be admitted on a permanent basis each year. However, this number includes immediate members of the immigrant's family who are also coming. So a head-of-household coming for a tech job and bringing a wife and two young children actually counts as four people.

Keeping families together

Family-based immigration has its limits, too. If a U.S. citizen or permanent resident wishes to bring their immediate family over, there are visas for this purpose. The number issued per year is based on a complicated formula devised by Congress, but is generally about half a million per given year. Family-based immigration is one of the heaviest areas of immigration. In 2014, family-based immigrants accounted for 64 percent of all new permanent residents in the United States.

>> Although there are stories of immigrant families being split up, in general the United States favors family-based immigration.

55

THE DIVERSITY VISA PROGRAM

The United States prides itself on being a melting pot of ethnicities and cultures. So, as part of the Immigration Act of 1990, the Diversity Visa lottery was established for countries that traditionally have a low rate of immigration to the United States. Under this program, 55,000 visas each year are randomly distributed to applicants from countries that have sent fewer than 50,000 immigrants to the United States over the previous 5 years.

Applicants for the program must have a high-school education or equivalent and must have worked for at least two years at a profession that requires at least two years of training or experience. Their professional experience must have occurred within the past five years. Spouses and unmarried children are also allowed to apply under this program.

REFUGEE PROTECTION

Refugees are people who come to the United States because they are fleeing persecution, or because their home country is unsafe due to natural disaster or violent conditions. If they are currently living in the United States and do not feel they can safely return to their home country, they are considered asylees.

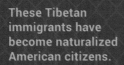

These Tibetan immigrants have become naturalized American citizens.

Each year, the government determines the number of refugees who will be allowed into the country. They decide which refugees will be granted entry based on many factors, such as whether they have family in the United States and whether they are a member of a potentially dangerous group.

REFUGEE ADMISSIONS FOR 2016

The Departments of State, Homeland Security, and Health and Human Services provide an example of the number of refugees allowed in a given year. In 2016, the president and Congress determined that the United States would allow:

- *25,000 refugees from Africa*
- *13,000 refugees from East Asia*
- *4,000 refugees from Europe and Central Asia*
- *3,000 refugees from Latin America and the Caribbean*
- *34,000 refugees from the Near East and South Asia*
- *6,000 refugees under an "unallocated reserve" quota*

This totals 85,000 refugees allowed in 2016.

ASYLUM

There is no specific quota established for people granted asylum. In 2014, 23,533 immigrants were granted asylum. Refugees and asylees have to meet the same criteria to obtain entry to the United States. The main difference is that an asylee is typically already residing in the United States when he or she requests asylum. A refugee typically applies as a refugee while still living in their home country.

CLOSING THE BORDERS?

With America's history as a "melting pot," it may seem surprising that immigration has been such a controversial topic in recent years. It was one of the most contentious issues of the presidential election in 2016. Both presidential candidates agreed that the current immigration system needed fixing, but their ideas for how to do so were drastically different.

Democratic presidential nominee Hillary Clinton argued for a comprehensive immigration reform that would provide a "pathway to full and equal citizenship" for immigrants. Clinton argued that doing so would repair broken immigrant families, bring immigrants into the formal economy, and ultimately strengthen national security.

Republican presidential nominee Donald Trump, on the other hand, argued for a clampdown on immigration. The slogan "Build the wall!" was often repeated during his campaign. It referred to his proposal that the United States build a physical, impenetrable wall along its border with Mexico, to keep out illegal immigrants. Trump also promised to strongly enforce immigration laws and immediately deport anyone in violation of them. He also vowed to end the practice of undocumented immigrants working in the United States.

President Donald Trump favors strict immigration laws and the immediate deportation of any undocumented immigrants who commit crimes.

Impact on the job market

Unemployment is, and always has been, an issue in the United States. Sometimes unemployment rates are low, and people are generally content—although even during the good times, there are always some people out of work. At other times, unemployment rates are sky-high, and American citizens live in fear of losing their jobs and not being able to provide for their families.

This fear often colors people's view of immigrants. If an American who has been out of work for months and is worried about providing for their family sees immigrants working in a similar job, it is not at all surprising that they would see it as immigrants taking jobs away from American people.

Are immigrants the problem?

In his 2016 bestselling memoir, *Hillbilly Elegy*, author J.D. Vance described his experience working in a working-class factory job in the Midwest. One of the things he noticed is the unwillingness of some Americans to work. He described natural-born American citizens who take a factory job and then do not show up to work, or take multiple extended breaks each day, or do personal business on work time. When they eventually lose their job, he described how they blame the government and refuse to accept responsibility for their loss.

Homeless encampments, like this one in California, may contain immigrants, but many natural-born American citizens as well.

Making a choice

Of course, Vance is only describing one segment of the population. His argument does not cover all Americans, or even all working-class Americans. He is pointing out that there may be more to the unemployment rate than immigrants accepting a job in the United States. If an employer has a choice between hiring an immigrant who is willing to put in the effort and do the work, or hiring a natural-born American who resents having to do hard labor and does not put in the effort, what should they choose?

National security

With the United States being a target of terrorist groups such as ISIS, American citizens are on edge. The attacks of September 11, 2001, showed that Americans cannot feel entirely safe, even in their own country. Since then, individuals claiming a connection to terrorist groups have carried out other attacks on U.S. soil.

Fear can lead to a knee-jerk reaction against immigrants. ISIS is a radical Islamist group, and the people who participate in it are Muslim. However, not all Muslims practice radical Islam. Just like Christianity has many denominations, so does Islam. The vast majority of Muslims are faithful, nonviolent people who would never carry out a terrorist attack.

Blaming Muslims

However, some American citizens fear that any Muslim could be a radical Islamist and could carry out a terrorist attack. To help prevent attacks, President Trump proposed a temporary ban on Muslims entering the United States. He also wanted to set up a registry for all Muslims living in the United States.

To some Americans, this is a good and logical solution. To others, it is similar to the Jewish registry Hitler established, and the ban on Asian immigrants in the 19th century. They also point out that many acts of violence are carried out by non-Muslims and natural-born U.S. citizens, so banning Muslim immigration would not stop attacks.

A Syrian group marched in Chicago in 2016 to raise awareness about the crisis in Syria. Many Syrian Muslims have sought refuge in the United States since the crisis.

THE FUTURE OF IMMIGRATION

The future of immigration is unknown. President Trump has already signed executive orders to begin building the wall on the Mexican border, to crack down on illegal immigration, and to deport any individuals found to be living in the United States without proper documentation.

Whatever happens, there will undoubtedly be more changes to come. The United States has a long history of changing immigration laws and ultimately remaining a melting pot of cultures.

GLOSSARY

abolitionists People who fought to end slavery.

anarchists People who believe in the absence of government.

anti-Semitism A hostility toward or prejudice against Jewish people.

aristocracy The highest class in society.

asylee A person seeking or granted political asylum.

Baltic states Three European countries on the eastern coast of the Baltic Sea: Estonia, Latvia, and Lithuania.

Bolshevik A member of the political party in Russia that preceded the Communist Party. Bolsheviks were considered radicals.

Calvinist A follower of the Protestant belief system espoused by John Calvin.

Cold War A period of tension between the United States and the Soviet Union that lasted from 1947 to 1991.

conquistador A Spanish conquerer.

displaced persons People who leave their homes in forced migration.

Dutch Republic A republic that existed from 1581 to 1795. It included the present-day countries of Belgium, the Netherlands, and Luxembourg.

English Separatists Protestants who were highly critical of the Church of England and wanted to separate from it.

forced labor Work that people are forced to do under the threat of punishment.

Great Depression A deep economic downturn from 1929 to 1939. Poverty and joblessness were at record highs.

Great Migration The mass migration of English citizens (mostly Puritans) to North America from 1630 to 1640.

green card A permit that allows an immigrant to live and work permanently in the United States.

headright system A system in which settlers were granted land for each indentured servant they brought in.

homogeneity Being all the same.

indentured servant An immigrant who was bound by contract to work for a specified period of time.

indigo A tropical plant that is the source of a dark blue dye.

melting pot A place where people of different backgrounds and cultures are mixed together.

naturalization The gaining of citizenship to a country.

potato blight A disease that attacks potatoes.

prospector A person who searched for gold during the Gold Rush.

proxy war A war initiated by a power that does not directly involve itself.

Puritans English Protestants who wanted to reform the Church of England and rid it of Catholic influence.

refugees People who have been forced to flee their country to avoid political danger, persecution, or natural disaster.

saboteurs People who engage in sabotage.

steerage The least expensive portion of a ship to have passage in.

Thirty Years' War A series of wars that took place in Central Europe over the period of 1618 to 1648.

visa A permit allowing a person to enter, leave, or stay in a country for a given period of time.

xenophobia Strong dislike or distrust of people from other countries.

FOR MORE INFORMATION

BOOKS

Baker, Brynn. *Life in America: Comparing Immigrant Experiences*. North Mankato, MN: Capstone Press, 2015.

Gjelten, Tom. *A Nation of Nations: A Great American Immigration Story*. New York, NY: Simon & Schuster, 2016.

Kravitz, Danny. *Journey to America: A Chronology of Immigration in the 1900s*. North Mankato, MN: Capstone Press, 2015.

WEBSITES

The National Park Service website features information about Natural Historic Landmarks that illustrate the history of the United States: **www.nps.gov/nhl/**

The Smithsonian National Museum of American History provides online exhibitions about U.S. history: **americanhistory.si.edu/exhibitions/online**

This website allows readers to search historic newspapers from 1789 to 1924: **kids.usa.gov/teens/history/us-history/index.shtml**

INDEX